RALPH RICHARDSON
A TRIBUTE

Ralph Richardson as Sergeant Fielding in
Bernard Shaw's *Too True to be Good*,
directed by H.K. Ayliff. Malvern Festival,
1932. Transfers to New Theatre.

RALPH RICHARDSON

A TRIBUTE

Devised and compiled by

ROBERT TANITCH

Evans

Published by Evans Brothers Limited,
Montague House, Russell Square,
London, WC1B 5BX

First published 1982

Designed and typeset by D P Press, Sevenoaks, Kent
and printed in Great Britain by B.A.S. Printers Limited
Over Wallop, Hampshire
ISBN 0 237 45680 X

This book is dedicated to Sir Ralph Richardson

*Ralph Richardson was born on the 19th of
December, 1902. He was knighted for his services
to theatre in 1947.*

1

1 Ralph Richardson makes his first professional appearance at the Marina Theatre, Lowestoft, in August 1921, with the Charles Doran Company. He plays Lorenzo in *The Merchant of Venice*.

2 Ralph Richardson as Mark Antony in Shakespeare's *Julius Caesar*. Charles Doran Company, touring 1923.

2

4

3

3 Ralph Richardson and Primrose Morgan in Eden Phillpotts' *The Farmer's Wife*, directed by H.K. Ayliff. The Birmingham Repertory Company, touring, 1925. Richardson plays Richard Coaker.

4 Stanley Lathury and Ralph Richardson in Leonid Andreyev's *He Who Gets Slapped*, directed by H.K. Ayliff. The Birmingham Repertory Company, 1926. Richardson plays a gentleman.

5

5 Ralph Richardson makes his first appearance on the London stage at the Scala Theatre on 10 July, 1926, in The Greek Play Society's production of Sophocles' *Oedipus at Colonus*, directed by Robert Atkins.

6 Viola Lyel, Ralph Richardson, Frank Vosper, Susan Richmond, Amy Veness, Alice and Drusilla Wills, Edward Petley and H.O. Nicholson in Eden and Adelaide Phillpotts' *Yellow Sands*, directed by H.K. Ayliff. Theatre Royal, Haymarket, 1926. Richardson plays Arthur Varwell.

6

7 Ralph Richardson, Clifford Marquand and Wallace Evennett in Shakespeare's *The Taming of the Shrew*, a modern-dress production, directed by H.K. Ayliff. Court Theatre, 1928. Richardson plays Tranio as a cockney chauffeur.

8 Ralph Richardson and Dorothy Turner in Harris Deans' *Aren't Women Wonderful?* directed by H.K. Ayliff. Court Theatre, 1928. Richardson plays Ben Hawley.

9 Ralph Richardson in the musical, *Silver Wings* by Dion Titheradge, Douglas Furber, Jack Waller and Joseph Tunbridge, directed by William Mollison. Dominion Theatre, 1930.

10 Ralph Richardson joins the Old Vic Company in 1930 and stays with them for two seasons until 1932. The company performs both at the Old Vic Theatre and Sadler's Wells.

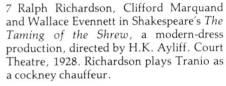

10

Billie, how is this for Caliban? Yellow and black. Ralph.

11

11 Ralph Richardson's sketch for his make-up as Caliban in Shakespeare's *The Tempest*, directed by Harcourt Williams. Old Vic Company, 1930.

12 Ralph Richardson as Don Pedro in Shakespeare's *Much Ado About Nothing*, directed by Harcourt Williams. Old Vic Company, 1931.

13

13 Robert Speaight as Malvolio, Harold Chapin as Sir Andrew Aguecheek and Ralph Richardson as Sir Toby Belch in Shakespeare's *Twelfth Night*, directed by Harcourt Williams. It is this Old Vic production which re-opens Sadler's Wells on 6 January, 1931.

14 Ralph Richardson as Matthew Merrygreek in Nicholas Udall's *Ralph Roister Doister*, directed by H.K. Ayliff. Malvern Festival, 1931 and 1932.

12

14

15

15 Ralph Richardson as Faulconbridge and Robert Speaight as John in Shakespeare's *King John*, directed by Harcourt Williams. Old Vic Company, 1931.

16 Phyllis Thomas as Kate, Ralph Richardson as Petruchio and Geoffrey Toone as a servant in Shakespeare's *The Taming of the Shrew*, directed by Harcourt Williams. Old Vic Company, 1931.

16

17

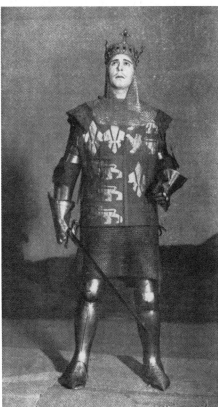

17 Robert Harris as Oberon, Phyllis Thomas as Titania, Ralph Richardson as Bottom and Leslie French as Puck in Shakespeare's *A Midsummer Night's Dream*, directed by Harcourt Williams. Old Vic Company, 1931.

18 Ralph Richardson as Shakespeare's *Henry V*, directed by Harcourt Williams. Old Vic Company, 1931.

19 Ralph Richardson as Ralph in Beaumont and Fletcher's *The Knight of the Burning Pestle*, directed by Harcourt Williams. Old Vic Company, 1932.

20 Alistair Sim as Lucilius, Ralph Richardson as Brutus, Robert Speaight as Cassius and Grenville Eves as Messala in Shakespeare's *Julius Caesar*, directed by Harcourt Williams. Old Vic Company, 1932.

18

19

20

21 Ralph Richardson and Grenville Eves in John Drinkwater's *Abraham Lincoln*, directed by John Drinkwater. Old Vic Company, 1932. Richardson plays General Grant.

22 Ralph Richardson as Iago and Edith Evans as Emelia in Shakespeare's *Othello*, directed by Harcourt Williams. Old Vic Company, 1932.

23/24 Robert Harris as Hamlet. Ralph Richardson as the Ghost and the First Grave-digger in Shakespeare's *Hamlet*, directed by Harcourt Williams. Old Vic Company, 1932.

22

25

25 Ralph Richardson, H.K. Ayliff, Ellen Pollock and Cedric Hardwicke in Bernard Shaw's *Too True to be Good*, directed by H.K. Ayliff. Malvern Festival, 1932. Transfers to New Theatre. Richardson plays the Bible and Buyan-reading Sergeant Fielding.

26 Flora Robson and Ralph Richardson in W. Somerset Maugham's *For Services Rendered*, directed by H.K. Ayliff. Globe Theatre, 1932. Richardson plays Collie Stratton who goes bankrupt and commits suicide.

26

Ralph Richardson and I are the same age and started our careers together in the same year in London after playing in repertory theatres outside of London. The play was by Somerset Maugham, but unfortunately out-of-date, as it was a 1920 'after the war play' and not done till 1930. Ralph and I used to worry and commiserate in the wings when we got an audience to laugh in the wrong place. I had to propose marriage to him as there was such a shortage of men! We thought we had spoiled the play.

Flora Robson

28   27

27 Dorothy Hyson, Kathleen Harrison, Anthony Bushell, Ralph Richardson and Cedric Hardwicke in *The Ghoul*, a horror film directed by T. Hayes Hunter. 1933.

28 Cecily Oates and Ralph Richardson in W. Somerset Maugham's last play, *Sheppey*, directed by John Gielgud. Wyndham's Theatre, 1933. Sheppey is a barber who wins a sweepstake and decides to put Christ's teachings into practice.

29 Ralph Richardson, Donald Calthrop and Jessie Matthews in *Friday the Thirteenth*, a multi-story film directed by Victor Saville. 1933. Richardson appears in the last episode as a schoolmaster in love with a chorus girl.

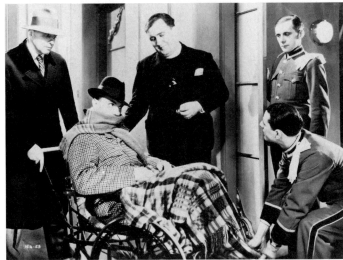

30 Ralph Richardson and Francis L. Sullivan in *The Return of Bulldog Drummond*, a film directed by Walter Summers. 1934. Richardson plays the hero.

31 Elizabeth Allan, Edmund Gwen, Anna May Wong, Ralph Richardson and John Loder in *Java Head*, a film directed by J. Walter Ruben. 1934. Richardson plays the son of an 1850s shipbuilder.

32

32 Ralph Richardson and Beatrix Lehmann in J.B. Priestley's *Eden End*, directed by Irene Hentschel. Duchess Theatre, 1934. Richardson plays the drunken actor, Charles Appleby.

33 Ralph Richardson and Marie Glory in *The King of Paris*, a film based on the life of Sacha Guitry, directed by Jack Raymond. 1934. Richardson plays an electrician who runs off with the matinee idol's girl.

33

34

*When I was a small boy, there was a well-known
and respected critic called J.T. Grein, who wrote
in one of his reviews: 'I hasten to the theatre as
to a rendezvous.' I am reminded of this happy
sentiment when I hasten – as to a rendezvous –
to any theatre in which Sir Ralph is playing.
And, of course, there's an added bonus if I am up
there with him.*

Raymond Huntley

34 Ralph Richardson as J.B. Priestley's
Cornelius, directed by Basil Dean. Duchess
Theatre, 1935. Cornelius is a businessman
who thinks there are more important things
in life than aluminium. Raymond Huntley
is in the cast.

35 Ralph Richardson and Jack Hulbert in
Bulldog Jack, a film directed by Walter
Forde. 1935. (American title: Alias Bulldog
Drummond.) Richardson now plays the
villain.

36

37

36 Maurice Evans as Romeo, Katharine Cornell as Juliet, Edith Evans as Nurse and Ralph Richardson as Mercutio in Shakespeare's *Romeo and Juliet*, directed by Guthrie McClintic. Martin Beck Theatre, New York, 1935.

37/38 Derek de Marney, Anthony Holles, Maurice Braddell, Ralph Richardson and Margaretta Scott in H.G. Wells' *Things to Come*, a film directed by William Cameron Menzies. 1936. Richardson plays the Boss, the fascist ruler of Everytown. Mussolini bans the film in Italy.

39 Madge Titheradge, Ralph Richardson, Edna Best and Robert Harris in Henri Bernstein's *Promise*, directed by Henri Bernstein. Shaftesbury Theatre, 1936. Richardson plays a scholarly, intellectual invalid.

40 Ralph Richardson and Laurence Olivier in J.B. Priestley's farcical tragedy, *Bees on the Boat Deck*, a political satire, which both actors direct. Lyric Theatre, 1936. They play two officers trying to stop everybody blowing up S.S. Gloriana, a tramp steamer.

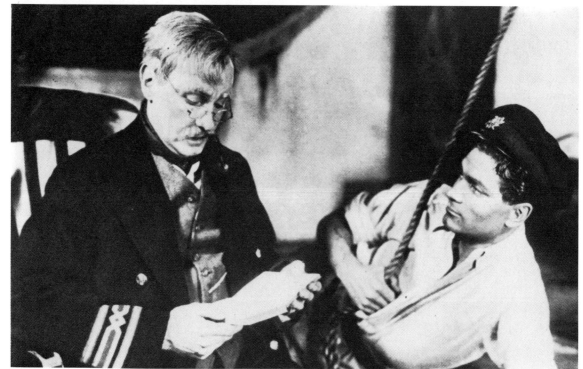

40

41 Edward Chapman, Ralph Richardson, Laurence Hanray and Wally Patch in H.G. Wells' *The Man Who Could Work Miracles*, a film directed by Lothar Mendes. 1936. Richardson plays Col. Winstanley.

42 Meriel Forbes, Hugh E. Wright, S. Victor Stanley and Ralph Richardson in Barré Lyndon's *The Amazing Dr Clitterhouse*, directed by Claud Gurney. Theatre Royal, Haymarket, 1936. Richardson plays Clitterhouse, masterminding a fur robbery. The role gives him his first big West End success.

42

43 Nigel Bruce, Ralph Richardson and Edward G. Robinson in *Thunder in the City*, a film directed by Marion Gering. 1937. Richardson plays a city banker who is hoodwinked by American salesmanship.

44 Diana Wynard and Ralph Richardson in Eugene Heltai's *The Silent Knight*, translated from the Hungarian by Humbert Wolfe into rhyming couplets and directed by Gilbert Miller. Richardson's leading role is largely silent.

45 Ralph Richardson as Bottom in Shakespeare's *A Midsummer Night's Dream*, directed by Tyrone Guthrie. Theatre Royal, Haymarket, 1937.

47　　　　　　　　　　　　　　46

46 Ralph Richardson and Binnie Barnes as Lord and Lady Mere in *The Divorce of Lady X*, a film directed by Tim Whelan. 1938.

47 Ralph Richardson and Harry Lomas in the film of Winifred Holtby's *South Riding*, directed by Victor Saville. 1938. Richardson plays Robert Carne, a country squire.

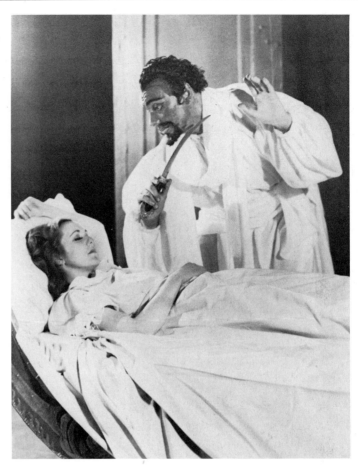

48 Curigwen Lewis as Desdemona and Ralph Richardson as Othello in Shakespeare's *Othello*, directed by Tyrone Guthrie. Old Vic, 1937. Laurence Olivier plays Iago.

49 Ralph Richardson and Robert Donat in the film of A.J. Cronin's *The Citadel*, directed by King Vidor. 1938. Richardson plays the drunken, idealistic Dr Denny.

50 Ralph Richardson as Robert Johnson in J.B. Priestley's modern morality play, *Johnson Over Jordan*, directed by Basil Dean. Saville Theatre, 1939.

51 The nightclub scene. Emma Trenchman as Madame Vulture. Masks designed by Elizabeth Haffenden.

52 Victoria Hopper and Ralph Richardson.

52

51

I am delighted to join in this birthday tribute to Sir Ralph Richardson, an old friend and my favourite actor, who has always given me in performance even more than I could give him. Nothing has ever been subtracted in his performance of any play of mine, but something rich and almost magical has always been added. Both as a dramatist and as a playgoer I have delighted in and blessed his range and depth.

Now that he has joined us old boys in the eighties, I beg him to keep going.

J.B. Priestley

53

53 Laurence Olivier and Ralph Richardson in *Q Planes*, a film directed by Tim Whelan. 1939. Richardson plays the scatterbrained secret serviceman. The film is re-issued during the war.

54 Captain Durrance discovers that he is blind. Ralph Richardson in the film of A.E.W. Mason's *The Four Feathers*, directed by Zoltan Korda. 1939.

Dearest Ralphie,

If life could provide another fifty-five years, I could not wish them more cause for pride, fellowship and love than has our joyous friendship given to me.

Your ever loving,

Larry

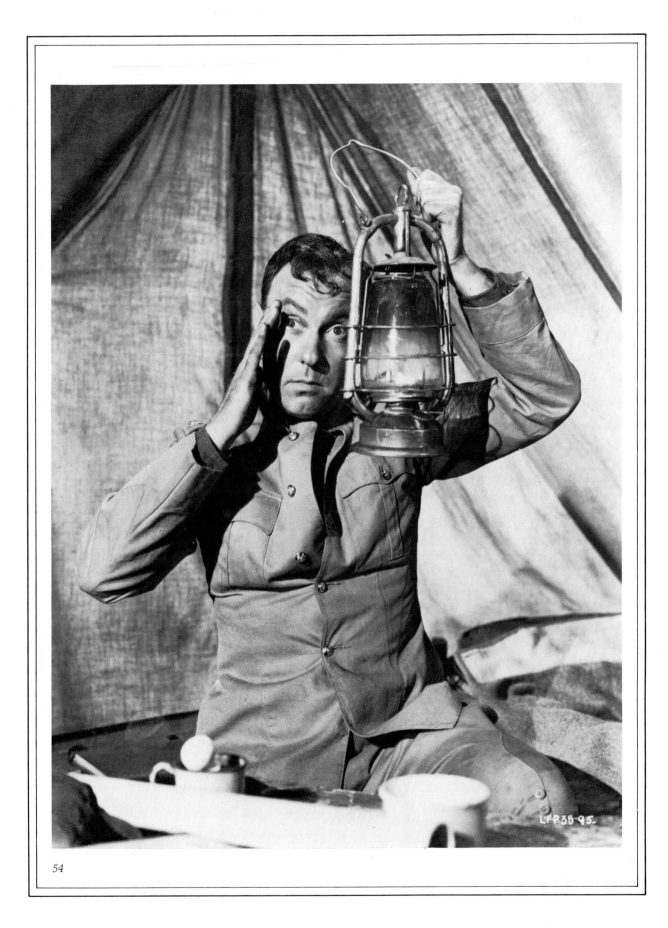

54

55 Ralph Richardson as a wing-commander in the RAF in *The Lion Has Wings*, a documentary film directed by Adrian Brunel, Brian Desmond Hurst and Michael Powell with the co-operation of the Air Ministry. 1939.

56 A barber is about to kill his blackmailer. Ralph Richardson and Romney Brent in *On The Night of the Fire*, a film directed by Brian Desmond Hurst. 1939. (American title: The Fugitive.)

57 Hugh Williams, Ralph Richardson and David Horne in *The Day Will Dawn*, a propaganda film directed by Harold French. 1942. (American title: The Avengers.) Richardson plays a journalist who is killed during the invasion.

58   59

58 Ralph Richardson as a Dutch patriot in *The Silver Fleet*, a propaganda film directed by Vernon Sewell. 1943.

59 Ralph Richardson and Pat McGrath in *The Volunteer*, a propaganda film directed by Michael Powell. 1943. Richardson plays himself.

From September 1939 to June 1944, Ralph Richardson serves in the Fleet Air Arm, rising to the rank of Lt-Commander RNVR. He is released from war service to act in and direct the Old Vic Company.

From 1944-1947 Ralph Richardson is joint director of the Old Vic Company with Laurence Olivier and John Burrell. The Company plays at the New Theatre.

60

60/61 Ralph Richardson as Peer and Sybil
Thorndike as Aase in Henrik Ibsen's *Peer
Gynt*, directed by Tyrone Guthrie and
Robert Helpmann. Old Vic Company,
1944. For his performance, Richardson is
awarded the Norwegian Medal of St Olav
by King Haakon.

61

62 Ralph Richardson as Bluntschli and Laurence Olivier as Sergius in Bernard Shaw's *Arms and the Man*, directed by John Burrell. Old Vic Company, 1944.

63 Ralph Richardson as Richmond and Laurence Olivier as Richard in Shakespeare's *Richard III*, directed by John Burrell. Old Vic Company, 1944.

Anton Chekhov's *Uncle Vanya*, directed by
John Burrell. Old Vic Company, 1945.

64 Sybil Thorndike as Nurse, Joyce
Redman as Sonya, Harcourt Williams as
the Professor, Ralph Richardson as Vanya
and Margaret Leighton as Yelena.

65 Laurence Olivier as Astrov, Ralph
Richardson and Joyce Redman.

65

66 Ralph Richardson as Falstaff and Laurence Olivier as Hotspur in Shakespeare's *Henry IV Part I,* directed by John Burrell. Old Vic Company, 1945.

67 Ralph Richardson as Falstaff and Joyce Redman as Doll Tearsheet in Shakespeare's *Henry IV Part II.*

*I just feel that he is a most noble gentleman, with this
wonderful charisma and magic. He was marvellously
helpful and encouraging to me in my early days in the
theatre, during that season at the New Theatre and
oh, so generous to act with. He has a marvellous
thing with young people, going out of his way to help
and encourage. I noticed this very much during the
latest time, playing at the National. What a great
privilege it has been for me to have known him and
acted with him. Surely the greatest Falstaff ever; and
for me, his Vanya, the most moving, on the edge of
laughter and tears, the nearest to Chaplin – I think
one of the greatest – the Chaplin of the theatre.*

Joyce Redman

68

69

68 Roy Jackson as the boy, Ralph Richardson as Tiresias, Nicholas Hannen as Chorus Leader and Laurence Olivier as Oedipus in Sophocles' *Oedipus*, directed by Michel Saint-Denis. Old Vic Company, 1945.

69 Ralph Richardson as Lord Burleigh and Laurence Olivier as Puff in Richard Brinsley Sheridan's *The Critic*, directed by Miles Malleson. Old Vic Company, 1945.

70 Julien Mitchell as Arthur Birling, Ralph Richardson as Inspector Goole, Harry Andrews as Gerald Croft and Alec Guinness as Eric Birling in J.B. Priestley's *An Inspector Calls*, directed by Basil Dean. Old Vic Company, 1946.

Ralph Richardson was an enormous encouragement to me when I came back to the theatre after the war and joined the Old Vic Company. He was hero and father to me in those days and I shall never forget his definitive Falstaff.

I remember one piece of advice he gave me which has always stood me in good stead; which was that he would always go on the set of the play just before the curtain went up and he would go round and touch all the props and the furniture in order to stimulate the reality and the emotion he was about to enact.

Harry Andrews

71 Ralph Richardson as Edmond Rostand's *Cyrano de Bergerac*, directed by Tyrone Guthrie. Old Vic Company, 1946.

72 Cecil Winter as Le Bret, Ralph Richardson, Margaret Leighton as Roxane and Nicholas Hannen as Ragueneau.

73 Margaret Leighton, Michael Warre as Christian and Ralph Richardson.

73

Ben Jonson's *The Alchemist*, directed by John Burrell. Old Vic Company, 1947

74 Ralph Richardson as Face and Joyce Redman as Dol Common.

75 Margaret Leighton as Dame Pliant, Peter Copley as Ananias, George Rose as Kastril, Michael Warre as Surly, Ralph Richardson, and George Relph as Subtle.

76/77 Margaret Leighton as Queen, Alec
Guinness as Richard and Ralph Richardson
as Gaunt in Shakespeare's *Richard II*,
directed by Ralph Richardson. Old Vic
Company, 1947.

77

78

79

78 Raymond Huntley and Ralph Richardson as two boffins in *School For Secrets*, a film directed by Peter Ustinov. 1946. (American title: Secret Flight.)

79 Ralph Richardson as Karenin and Vivien Leigh as Anna in the film of Lev Tolstoy's *Anna Karenina*, directed by Julien Duvivier. 1948.

80 Ralph Richardson returns to the West End stage in Romilly Cavan's *Royal Circle*, directed by himself. Wyndham's Theatre, 1948. Richardson plays a Ruritanian king.

80

81

82

81/82 Ralph Richardson, Michele Morgan
and Bobby Henrey in Graham Greene's
The Fallen Idol, a film directed by Carol
Reed. 1948. Richardson plays the
ambassador's butler who is suspected of
murder.

83 Peggy Ashcroft as Catherine and Ralph
Richardson as Dr Sloper in *The Heiress*, the
Ruth and Augustus Goetz adaptation of
'Washington Square' by Henry James,
directed by John Gielgud. Theatre Royal,
Haymarket, 1949.

84 Miriam Hopkins as Lavinia Penniman, Montgomery Clift as Morris Townsend, Ralph Richardson as Dr Sloper and Olivia de Havilland as Catherine in *The Heiress*, the film directed by William Wyler. 1949. Richardson is nominated for an Academy award.

I have the keenest admiration for his work and marvel still at his splendid performance in The Heiress. *He is an artist of great style and precision – a master, really. It astounds me, however, to learn that he is soon to be eighty! He will adorn the age and carry it off with the very flair which characterizes his performances – of that we can all be sure.*

Olivia de Havilland

I have always found Ralph the most magical of actors – not always easy to play with – but I never failed to watch and listen from 'the side of the stage' long before I was needed there. Oh, the magic and the charm!

Wendy Hiller

85 A bank clerk, suffering from amnesia, is questioned by the police about a theft and a murder. Ralph Richardson and Campbell Singer in R.C. Sherriff's *Home At Seven*, directed by Murray Macdonald. Wyndham's Theatre, 1950.

86

87

Anton Chekhov's *Three Sisters*, directed by Peter Ashmore. Aldwych Theatre, 1951.

86 Isolde Denham as a maid, Frances Waring as Anfissa, Ralph Richardson as Vershinin, Celia Johnson as Olga, Eric Porter as Solyoni, Walter Hudd as Kuligin, Diana Churchill as Natasha, Michael Warre as Andrey and Harcourt Williams as Cheboutikin.

87 Robert Beaumont as Touzenbach, Renne Asherson as Irina, Ralph Richardson, Margaret Leighton as Masha and Walter Hudd.

89   88

88 Wendy Hiller as Mrs Almayer, Robert Morley as Almayer, Ralph Richardson as Captain Lingard and Trevor Howard as Willems in Joseph Conrad's *An Outcast of the Islands*, a film directed by Carol Reed. 1951.

89 Jack Hawkins, Ralph Richardson and Margaret Leighton in the film of R.C. Sherriff's *Home at Seven*, directed by Ralph Richardson. 1952. (American title: Murder on Monday.)

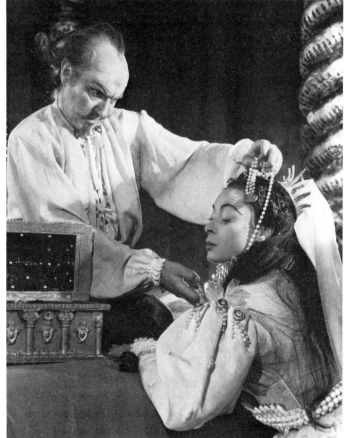

91 92

Shakespeare Memorial Theatre, Stratford-upon-Avon, 1952.

90 Ralph Richardson as Prospero and Margaret Leighton as Ariel in Shakespeare's *The Tempest*, directed by Michael Benthall.

91 Ralph Richardson and Margaret Leighton as Macbeth and Lady Macbeth in Shakespeare's *Macbeth*, directed by John Gielgud.

92 Ralph Richardson as Volpone and Siobhan McKenna as Celia in Ben Jonson's *Volpone*, directed by George Devine.

It is difficult to imagine that Ralph has an eightieth birthday. He always seems eternally young and to be laughing at his own private understanding of life.

I met him for the first time in the film, Bulldog Drummond. I am a bit hazy about this film, but I do remember Ralph throwing me over an extremely high barbed wire fence and I fell and sprained my ankle and couldn't work for some time afterwards. Then came the film, South Riding, in which I played his young mad wife. It was a small part but everyone always remembers the scene when I rode upstairs on a horse and hit Ralph fiercely over the head with a riding crop! I don't know how worried Ralph was, but the horse and I were terrified. After that, we were together again in David Lean's The Sound Barrier. I played his daughter. He was so marvellous in this film.

I have only been with him once on the stage. That was in Promise. Again I had only one short scene but I used to stand in the wings and watch him playing scenes with Edna Best. In fact I was pregnant during the run of this play and one night I fainted after making my exit from the stage. I remember how kind Ralph was when he picked me up and helped me through my shame and embarrassment; but then he is so full of compassion and to me this comes through so strongly in his acting. How lovely for him, that we all love him so much.

Ann Todd

94

95

93 Ralph Richardson and Ann Todd in Terence Rattigan's *The Sound Barrier*, a film directed by David Lean. 1952. (American title: Breaking The Sound Barrier). Richardson plays the millionaire aircraft designer and manufacturer.

94 Ralph Richardson and Denholm Elliott in the film of Wynyard Browne's stage play, *The Holly and the Ivy*, directed by George More O'Farrall. 1952. Richardson plays the Reverend Martin Gregory in whom his children find it impossible to confide.

95 Ralph Richardson and Meriel Forbes in R.C. Sherriff's *The White Carnation*, directed by Noel Willman. Globe Theatre, 1953. Richardson plays a very solid stockbroker ghost who, while haunting his old house, gradually realizes he is dead.

96

97

Sir Ralph is loved so much and admired by all, both in and out of the profession. I have been privileged to work with him in the theatre, on television, and on film.

When I was with him for the first time in A Day by the Sea. *I was very much in awe of him, and as we were running through the marvellous scene I had with him, I asked if he thought I should do a line this way, or another. He gave me a piece of advice I have followed for the rest of my working life. He said, 'Don't let's talk about it, let's just do it.'*

That to me sums up the magic of this great instinctive actor. I feel honoured to have known him.

Megs Jenkins

96 Dr Farley turns down Miss Matheison's offer of marriage. Ralph Richardson and Megs Jenkins in *A Day by the Sea*.

97 Lewis Casson, John Gielgud, Patricia Laurence, Ralph Richardson, Sybil Thorndike and Irene Worth in N.C. Hunter's *A Day by the Sea*, directed by John Gielgud. Theatre Royal, Haymarket, 1953.

98 Meriel Forbes and Ralph Richardson as chorus girl and Grand Duke in Terence Rattigan's occasional fairy tale, *The Sleeping Prince*, directed by Lionel Harris. The play tours Australia and New Zealand in 1955.

Ralph once said to me: 'Rehearsing a part is like chasing a beautiful woman through a maze of corridors. Just as you reach to grab her by the skirts and you think you've got her, she's turned a corner and she's gone.'

For me no actor is so satisfying to watch in rehearsal or performance. He is immensely hard-working and concentrates on every minute detail. He can bring to a line a depth and a meaning which illuminates it to so great an extent that you feel you need to re-read the whole text. Watching him, as I have done frequently, one feels he could breathe life into a stone. Much of his observation is instinctive.

Terence Rattigan said of his performance in Separate Tables *that watching Ralph at work made him understand his own play and realize more fully what his writing contained.*

Ralph is a shy man, who never seeks the limelight. I consider him to be one of the true 'greats' of our time: a man of great sensitivity, humility, originality and generosity. He is totally without affectation and is unpretentious. If I paint a picture of many virtues, let me add that Ralph is quite unaware of them.

Lionel Harris

99 Ralph Richardson and Meriel Forbes in Terence Rattigan's *Separate Tables*, directed by Lionel Harris. The play tours Australia and New Zealand in 1955. Richardson plays Major Pollock, a bogus major, who has committed an offence in a cinema and got his name into the local newspaper.

100 'I am not in the giving vein today.'
Gloucester, newly-crowned, rejects
Buckingham. Laurence Olivier and Ralph
Richardson in the film of Shakespeare's
Richard III, directed by Laurence Olivier.
1955.

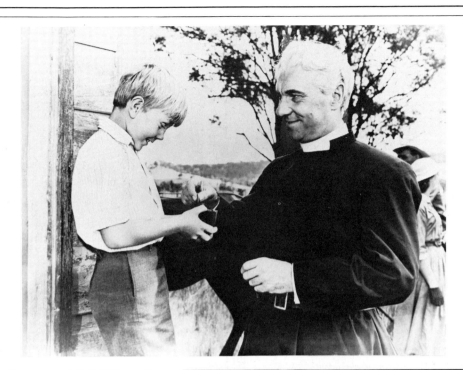

101

101 Colin Petersen and Ralph Richardson in *Smiley*, a film set in the Australian bush and directed by Anthony Kimmins. 1956.

102 Ralph Richardson as Timon and Dudley Jones as Apemantus in Shakespeare's *Timon of Athens*, directed by Michael Benthall. Old Vic. 1956.

102

103 Ralph Richardson as General St Pé in Jean Anouilh's *The Waltz of the Toreadors*, directed by Harold Clurman. Coronet Theatre, New York, 1957. The General is a compulsive womaniser, living with his invalid, bed-ridden wife.

104 Carlo Justini, Ralph Richardson and Margaret Leighton in *The Passionate Stranger*, a film directed by Muriel Box. 1957. (American title: A Novel Affair). Richardson plays the husband of an authoress and a character in her novel.

104

Ralph Richardson is quite unlike any other human being. In private as well as in public life he is unique.

In work he is fascinated with the craft of acting, just as in life he is fascinated with the craft of clock-making. The satisfaction and pleasure he can get at rehearsals from certain passages in a script which demand elaborate technical accomplishment, particularly of a physical nature, are things I have never encountered to the same extent in fifty years in the theatre. Maybe in a former life he was a clown in the Commedia dell' Arte – or a magician on the halls.

Like Edith Evans, he will reject some effect in the text which has been carefully worked out by an author, in favour of some imaginative fancy of his own, leaving that author wondering whether he ought not to have thought of it Ralph's way to start with. He makes his own rules. (We play along with them!). Is this one way of describing genius? Maybe.

Robert Bolt once said to me: 'When you've once been associated with Ralph, you'll never be quite the same again!' This was not intended to be a back-handed compliment but a statement of fact. I personally learnt a lot from our association – not least to avoid talking too much (and too directly!) at rehearsals, for it is not possible to analyse the magic distilled by Ralph when he is on form. It is a mystery and a marvel.

105   *Frith Banbury*

106

105 Ralph Richardson and Andrew Ray in Robert Bolt's *Flowering Cherry*, directed by Frith Banbury. Theatre Royal, Haymarket, 1957. The play runs for over 400 performances. Richardson plays Cherry, whose whole life is a lie; even his day-dreams are lies.

106 Ralph Richardson and Susan Burnet in *Flowering Cherry*.

I have very many memories of Ralph stored away from the eighteen months I spent with him in Flowering Cherry *from 1957 onwards. But I think what I remember most is when I went to the side of the stage during one matinee late on in the run to watch Ralph and Susan Burnet (the girl I was later to marry) playing a scene. I was moved to tears by Ralph's performance. Apart from his power as an actor, he also has such gentleness and sensitivity as an actor. I learned a great deal from him. I have never experienced, since, being in a play with anyone for so long who could still move me in such a way.*

Andrew Ray

I have worked only once with him and that over twenty years ago, but I have, of course, admired him for far longer than that. One of the most striking things about him is the extraordinary extent of the affection with which he is spoken of by members of the acting profession. Actors love to imitate his vocal characteristics. There is always a Ralph story, richly flavoured with the recollection of his particular and unique warmth, and always told with a loving appreciation.

At one period of his acting life, around the time he was playing in Home at Seven *he was always described as the epitome of 'the man in the street' by critics and such. This seemed a very limited view of his personality which for me has always contained the Merlin qualities of pure wizardry. And yet, at one and the same time, he is the voice, not only of ordinary man, but of humanity, both recognizable and rare. He has an immense concentration which he seems to take up and hold like a baton or a wand, only to relinquish it when the curtain falls.*

Any play in which he appears is subjected to the disciplines of his own and very personal and strong sense of rhythm. Other performers must submit to it or flounder – and of course, we do submit and find ourselves carried inexorably along on the current of his tough and dazzling talent.

I am very grateful that I have worked with him and that I know him.

Paul Scofield

107 Oliver Burt, Gerald Flood, Phyllis Calvert, Ralph Richardson and Paul Scofield in Graham Greene's *The Complaisant Lover*, directed by John Gielgud. Globe Theatre, 1959. Richardson plays a boring dentist.

109   108

108 Maurice Denham, Ralph Richardson and Noël Coward in the film of Graham Greene's *Our Man in Havana*, directed by Carol Reed. 1960. Richardson plays the chief of the British secret service.

109 Ralph Richardson as Sir Edward Carson, Counsel for the prosecution, in *Oscar Wilde*, a film directed by Gregory Ratoff. 1960. Robert Morley plays Wilde.

110 Hazel Terry, Robert Tunstall, Ralph Richardson and Robin Hawdon in Enid Bagnold's *The Last Joke*, directed by Glen Byam Shaw. Phoenix Theatre, 1960. Richardson plays a millionaire.

110

Of all the actors, the older and more experienced actors I worked with in my early years, Ralph had the greatest effect on me. Indeed it was seeing his Falstaff at the age of ten that determined me upon a stage career. I think it still the greatest piece of acting I've ever seen. The histrionics of it amaze me as I think of it now. That wonderful ability to hold the contradictions of the character in such harmony that it ceases to be 'acting' on any level at all. I count it the rarest of privileges to have been given the opportunity to work with him.

Daniel Massey

111

112

113

111 'Lady Teazle, by all that's damnable!'
Anna Massey as Lady Teazle, Daniel
Massey as Charles Surface, Ralph
Richardson as Sir Peter Teazle and John
Neville as Joseph Surface in Richard
Brinsley Sheridan's *The School For
Scandal*, directed by John Gielgud. Theatre
Royal, Haymarket, 1962. Tours America,
opening in New York in 1963.

112 Eva Marie Saint, Peter Lawford and
Ralph Richardson in *Exodus*, a film
directed by Otto Preminger. 1960.
Richardson plays a British officer in charge
of a Jewish refugee camp in Cyprus.

113 Ralph Richardson as Themistocles in
The 300 Spartans, a film directed by
Rudolph Maté. 1962.

114 Ralph Richardson as James Tyrone and Katharine Hepburn as Mary Cavan Tyrone in the film of Eugene O'Neill's *Long Day's Journey Into Night*, directed by Sydney Lumet. 1962.

Sir Ralph is unique, a delicious actor, a remarkable personality, a generous human being, and to do a play with him – in my case O'Neill's Long Day's Journey into Night *– was an opportunity I'm glad that I did not miss.*

Katharine Hepburn

Ralph and I worked on Long Day's Journey into Night. *I tend to be a little long-winded and one day finished eleven minutes of an answer to a short question of Ralph's. He looked at me balefully and said: 'Ah, I think I know what you want – a little more flute and a little less cello.' From then on – working together was joyful. He basically didn't like acting in movies, but I think he had a creative time.*

In my view, he is, perhaps, the foremost actor in the English-speaking world. The depth, perception, and human humor that permeates everything, reveals everything that we are to us.

Sidney Lumet

115 Ralph Richardson and Dean Stockwell as Edmund Tyrone in Eugene O'Neill's *Long Day's Journey Into Night.*

116 'There's no danger as long as I keep silent.' Ralph Richardson as Judge Brack and Ingrid Bergman as Hedda in Henrik Ibsen's *Hedda Gabler*, directed for television by Alex Segal. BBC/CBS 1962.

117 Ralph Richardson as Sir Stanley Johnson, the newly-appointed Minister of Labour, in Terence Rattigan's television play, *Heart to Heart*, directed by Alvin Rakoff, which is the first play to be commissioned for 'the largest theatre in the world'. BBC 1962.

Sir Ralph is, as everyone who knows him will tell you, a very special person and his qualities as an actor make him unique. I particularly enjoy his poetry-reading, which I can only describe as complicatedly simple. *This sounds like a contradiction in terms, but, having worked with him in Shakespeare, I know that an immense amount of work and thought goes towards producing the effect of spontaneity. His reading of Blake's* The Lamb *is, to my mind, a good example of this and also of his musicality, which is achieved without sounding in the least 'precious': he has 'the bowing' – one of his own phrases – of a great string player.*

I shall never forget playing with him in Six Characters in Search of An Author *in 1963. His stepfather was definitely not of this world: in the scene which shows him visiting his stepdaughter in the bordello – I played her – he gave the* impression *of touching me in the most lascivious way without actually doing so. We were supposed to be creatures of a sort of half-world, of the imagination of the author. I cannot imagine any other actor achieving that effect so completely and with such economy.*

Barbara Jefford

118 Ralph Richardson and Barbara Jefford in Luigi Pirandello's *Six Characters in Search of an Author*, the opening production of the Mayfair Theatre, directed by William Ball. 1963. Richardson plays the stepfather.

119 Ralph Richardson, Gina Lollobrigida and Sean Connery in *Woman of Straw*, a film directed by Basil Dearden. 1964. Richardson plays a sadistic tycoon.

118

119

120 Ralph Richardson and Jane Birkin in Graham Green's *Carving a Statue*, directed by Peter Wood. Theatre Royal, Haymarket, 1964. Richardson plays 'a not very good sculptor'.

121 Alec Guinness, Geraldine Chaplin, Ralph Richardson and Omar Sharif in the film of Boris Pasternak's *Dr Zhivago*, directed by David Lean. 1965. Richardson plays Alexander Gromeko.

122 Ralph Richardson, Michael Hordern, Hugh Williams and Alexander Knox in *Khartoum*, a film directed by Basil Dearden. 1966. Richardson plays Gladstone.

123 Ralph Richardson and John Mills as the last surviving members of a tontine in the film of Robert Louis Stevenson's *The Wrong Box*, directed by Bryan Forbes. 1966.

120   121

122

I have known and admired Sir Ralph Richardson for many years, but I have only had the pleasure and privilege of acting with him on one occasion. This was in a film called The Wrong Box. I was slightly diffident about this project, as during the first scene I was required to try and kill the great man by garrotting him, stabbing him and poisoning him. But he was so easy to work with, and generous and enthusiastic, that I think I enjoyed the few days that it took to shoot the scene as much as anything I had ever done in fifty years in the profession.

John Mills

123

124 Cyril Luckham as Finch M'Comas and
Ralph Richardson as the Waiter in Bernard
Shaw's *You Never Can Tell*, directed by
Glen Byam Shaw. Theatre Royal,
Haymarket, 1966.

Sir Ralph is always surprising. Whether life surprises him, I don't know, but if a star danced when Ellen Terry was born, I think one winked at Sir Ralph's arrival, and he has twinkled ever since.

In a TV interview, asked whether his recent knighthood had changed his life, he replied -- after one of those immensely long, yet somehow charged pauses that must be the hallmark of greatness – that afterwards, at luncheon, he had found a pearl in his oyster. This, to me, is his charm, that he always finds the unexpected angle. And pearls in oysters, of course.

I played with him at the Theatre Royal, Haymarket, in You Never Can Tell, *one of Shaw's Plays Pleasant, made pleasanter still by Sir Ralph's enchanting performance as William, the waiter, who presides over the sea-side hotel in which the play is set. His appearance was wonderfully thought out: the moon face over the floppy bow tie, the slightly bent knees, the sagging trousers wrinkling at the ankles. His stage effects looked effortless, but were most carefully created; the lunch party scene, in which William unobtrusively steers the conversation whilst deftly replacing the soup course with the fish, took nearly three weeks to get right – but once right, it stayed right. The soup and the fish, by the way, were quite good; just as the tea in Act 3 was always hot; and best of all, the music in the carnival scene was played live by a trio, instead of being recorded on tape. This was Ralph's idea, I was told. After we had danced off under the coloured lights to the strains of this little band, he would regale listeners in the wings with accounts of how he had danced with Fred Astaire, completely convincing the younger members of the cast, who only began to doubt him when he extended the claim to Nijinsky.*

The whole production was stamped with the Richardson style, on-stage and off. For example, by his wish, we were given our calls by a call-boy tapping on the door, instead of an impersonal voice over the tannoy. I am sure that if sea-side rock had been on sale at the resort in which the play is set, it would have had 'R.R.' stamped all the way through! Only once was his concern for detail misdirected. In one scene I had to pour out tea, and whoever set the tray always put the pot with the handle facing away from me, making it very awkward to grasp. I asked if it could be set the other way round, and the next night this was done, but 'O-oh, dear!' cried Sir Ralph as he put the tray down in front of me. 'Someone has moved the tea-pot!' And he carefully lifted it and put it back in the old position, with such kind solicitude, I hadn't the heart to get it changed again; and for the rest of my days as Mrs Clandon, it remained the wrong way round.

Judy Campbell

The March Hare

Memories of working with Ralph Richardson are a pot-pourri of eccentricities and absent-mindedness, mixed up with a fiercely concentrated technique and dazzling idiosyncratic style.

But what fun to be in a Company with him. Peering through the peep-hole at a few empty seats, 'I see Mr and Mrs Wood are in front!'; passing him on the stairs – adjusting his lace cuffs, and patting his feathered tricorne, 'Is it safe to go down, cocky?' (as though the audience were manning machine-guns); chatting in his dressing-room – he in his burgundy velvet coat and breeches, wigless, pipe in mouth and parrot on shoulder, like an upmarket Long John Silver, neatly side-stepping Jose's droppings on the carpet, 'Are you fond of Dr Gordon's?' as he passed me the gin bottle; he is a private man, a shy man. And a lovable man.

He is a fanatic about props. In You Never Can Tell *he had a short entrance, and exit, to make – simply carrying a large silver tray loaded with afternoon tea. He had only to take on the tray, set it down with a Shavian quip, and leave. I was waiting in the wings for my scene one evening and caught Ralph staring at the tray in dismay. 'Oh! Oh! Oh!' he was crying, 'Celia Bannerman has eaten a biscuit!' I pointed out there were still plenty of biscuits on the plate. 'But the pattern, old fellow, the pattern! It's gone!'*

In The Rivals *I wanted to make my first Bob Acres entrance carrying a dead hare as a surprise for Jack Absolute. There was some problem about dealing with the hare after my scene. I was going to take it off with me when a voice called to Glen Byam Shaw, 'No, no Glenny – leave the rabbit!' Ralph's scene followed mine and he was terribly disappointed that he could never find a satisfactory way of using such an unusual prop. He tried sitting on it; he tried chucking it on the fire in mistake for a log. Nothing worked and he had to abandon it. To this day he asks me 'Where's the rabbit?'*

Years later, at a party I gave in New York with Tony Shaffer, as the din was at its loudest, Ralph's wife – the beautiful Meriel Forbes – said, 'Where's Ralph? I think we ought to go, it's so late.' I had last seen him in the discotheque room we'd set up. He was in animated conversation with Andy Warhol and his latest Superstar Jackie (I'm-not-a-girl-I'm-not-a-boy-I'm-just-Jackie) Curtis. But now Ralph had disappeared. John Gielgud said, 'Oh! Ralph's in the sitting-room behind the curtains.' I walked through the crowded room. A pair of legs protruded below the folds of the curtain. Ralph was sitting by himself, wrapped in the curtain, looking across the reservoir to the lights of Manhattan. 'It's time to go, Ralph,' I said. 'Where's the rabbit?' he replied.

Keith Baxter

125

126

125 Margaret Rutherford as Mrs Malaprop, Ralph Richardson as Sir Anthony Absolute and Daniel Massey as Jack Absolute in Richard Brinsley Sheridan's *The Rivals*, directed by Glen Byam Shaw. Theatre Royal, Haymarket, 1966.

126 Ralph Richardson as Clarence, 9th Earl of Emsworth, in the TV adaptation of P.G. Wodehouse's *Blandings Castle*, produced for television by Michael Mills. BBC 1967.

127

128

129

127 Ralph Richardson as Shylock in Shakespeare's *The Merchant of Venice*, directed by Glen Byam Shaw. Theatre Royal, Haymarket, 1967.

128 Sheila Reid as Maria and Ralph Richardson as Sir Toby Belch in Shakespeare's *Twelfth Night*, directed for television by John Dexter. ATV 1968.

129 Ralph Richardson, Kenneth More and Ian Holm in the film of Joan Littlewood and Charles Chilton's *Oh! What a Lovely War*, directed by Richard Attenborough. 1969. Richardson plays Sir Edward Grey.

131 130

130 Coral Browne, Hayward Morse, Ralph Richardson, Julia Foster and Stanley Baxter in Joe Orton's posthumous *What The Butler Saw*, directed by Robert Chetwyn. Queen's Theatre, 1969. Richardson plays Dr Rance, who runs a mad-house.

131 Ralph Richardson and Fred Astaire in *Midas Run*, a film directed by Alf Kjellin. 1969. (English title: A Run on Gold) Richardson plays a secret serviceman.

132 Michael Hordern and Ralph Richardson in the film of John Antrobus and Spike Milligan's *the bed-sitting-room*, directed by Dick Lester. 1969. Richardson plays Lord Fortnum of Alamein.

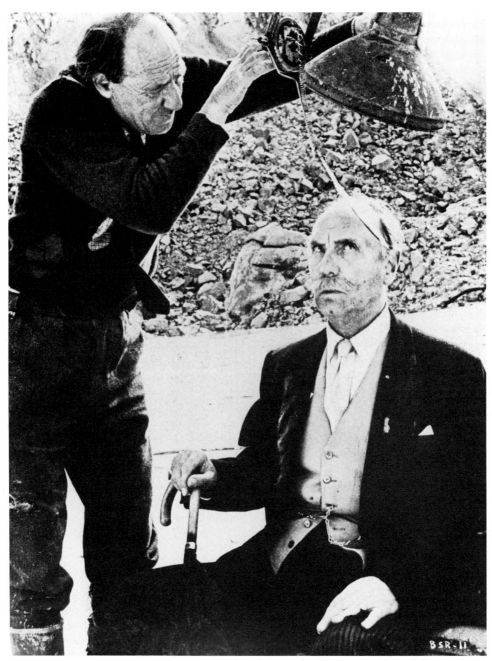

132

I treasure the memory of playing a scene with him, sitting on an enormous pile of old boots at the bottom of a Cornish china clay pit, in Dick Lester's film of the bed-sitting room. He was a gloriously eccentric post-bomb Prime Minister; and it's for his eccentricities that we love him, of course, motor-bike and all.

Michael Hordern

133

133 Ralph Richardson as the head of the secret service in the film of John Le Carré's *The Looking Glass War*, directed by Frank R. Pierson. 1969.

134 Ralph Richardson as David Kelly, the British Minister in Switzerland, and Curt Jurgens as Baron von Richter in *Battle of Britain*, a film directed by Guy Hamilton. 1969.

135 Edith Evans as Aunt Betsey, Robin Phillips as David Copperfield, Ralph Richardson as Micawber and Susan Hampshire as Agnes Wickfield in the film of Charles Dickens' *David Copperfield*, directed by Delbert Mann. 1969.

134

135

136 Ralph Richardson and John Gielgud as two inmates of a mental institution in David Storey's *Home*, directed by Lindsay Anderson. Royal Court, 1970. Transfers to Apollo Theatre and later to the Morosco Theatre, New York. Richardson is awarded the Evening Standard Best Actor Award.

Sir Ralph Richardson is one of my oldest and dearest friends and colleagues. We first met and worked together at the Old Vic in the 1930 season, and have acted together many times, most recently in David Storey's Home *and Harold Pinter's* No Man's Land. *I also directed him in several plays:* Sheppey *by Somerset Maugham (1934) Henry James'* The Heiress, The School for Scandal, Macbeth *and* A Day by the Sea *by N.C. Hunter.*

By his unique personality and dedicated professionalism he has lent immense distinction and originality throughout his brilliant career in a succession of fine performances both on stage and screen.

John Gielgud

137 Dandy Nichols and Ralph Richardson
in David Storey's *Home*.

'Look here,' the conjuror says, 'nothing up my
sleeve: nothing in my hand,' and, having hitched
up the one and shown you the palm of the other,
he produces from behind your ear a playing card,
a bird, a length of variegated coloured ribbon,
and then, stepping back a pace or two, adds,
'Nothing in my hat,' tips the inside in your
direction – empty – tips it upright once again,
takes out the proverbial rabbit, continues,
'Nothing inside my jacket,' shows you the lining
and, from inside the breast pocket, extracts . . .

At least, this is the image that often occurs to me
as I sit across the rehearsal-room floor and watch
the poet producing, from the air around, the
substance of his vision.

Congratulations on his eightieth year!

David Storey

138 Corin Redgrave and Ralph Richardson in James Elroy Flecker's *Hassan*, directed for television by Rex Tucker. BBC 1971. Richardson plays the title role.

139 Ralph Richardson as Mr Hardcastle and Juliet Mills as Kate Hardcastle in Oliver Goldsmith's *She Stoops to Conquer*, directed for television by Michael Elliott. BBC 1971.

140 Michael Gothard, Ralph Richardson and Shelley Winters in *Whoever Slew Auntie Roo?* a film updating the Hansel and Gretel story and directed by Curtis Harrington. 1971. (American title: Who Slew Auntie Roo?) Richardson plays a bogus medium.

141 John Gielgud and Ralph Richardson in *Eagle in a Cage*, a film directed by Fielder Cook. 1971. Richardson plays Sir Hudson Lowe, Governor of St Helena and Napoleon's jailor.

138   139

140

141

142 Ralph Richardson, Jill Bennett and Sheila Ballantine in John Osborne's *West of Suez*, directed by Anthony Page. Royal Court, 1971. Transfers to Cambridge Theatre. Richardson plays a distinguished writer, living in the Caribbean, who is finally shot by revolutionaries.

143 John Gielgud, Ralph Richardson, Mona Washbourne and Dandy Nichols in the television production of David Storey's *Home*, directed by Lindsay Anderson. BBC 1972.

144 Satan disguised as a monk. Ralph Richardson in *Tales from the Crypt*, a film directed by Freddie Francis. 1972.

145 Ralph Richardson as the Caterpillar in the film of Lewis Carroll's *Alice's Adventures in Wonderland*, directed by William Sterling. 1972.

146 John Mills, Jon Finch and Ralph Richardson in *Lady Caroline Lamb*, a film written and directed by Robert Bolt. 1972. Richardson plays George III.

142

143

144

145

146

147

148

147 Ralph Richardson in William Douglas Home's *Lloyd George Knew My Father*, directed by Robin Midgley. Savoy Theatre, 1972. Australia, 1973. North America, 1974. Richardson plays General Sir William Boothroyd who, learning that his wife intends to commit suicide, does nothing to dissuade her.

148 Ralph Richardson as Dr Rank in a film of Henrik Ibsen's *A Doll's House*, directed by Patrick Garland. 1973.

149 Ralph Richardson and Michael Sarrazin in *Frankenstein: The True Story*, a film made for television, directed by Jack Smight. 1973. Richardson plays an old, blind hermit who offers the Creature sanctuary and friendship.

149

150/151 Malcolm McDowell and Ralph Richardson in the film, *O Lucky Man,* from the novel by David Sherwin, directed by Lindsay Anderson. 1973. Richardson plays two roles: the enormously rich and ruthless tycoon and a poor tailor.

150

Do Ralph Richardsons' performances – each a work of high, idiosyncratic art – dazzle by the magic of supreme professionalism? Or by the professionalism of the supreme magician? Both, naturally. Humble and arrogant, certain and unsure, conscious and inspired, he is the director's torment and delight. All other secrets must remain in confidence – between friends.

Lindsay Anderson

151

152

152 Ralph Richardson as Borkman and Peggy Ashcroft as Ella Rentheim in Henrik Ibsen's *John Gabriel Borkman*, directed by Peter Hall. The National Theatre at The Old Vic, 1975.

153 Michael Feast as Foster, Ralph Richardson as Hirst, Terence Rigby as Briggs and John Gielgud as Spooner in Harold Pinter's *No Man's Land*, directed by Peter Hall. The National Theatre at The Old Vic, 1975. Transfers to Wyndham's Theatre and then goes to New York in 1976. Richardson plays a wealthy author who is protected by two sinister bodyguards.

Three great privileges:

Firstly, to have seen Ralph Richardson, actor, from the 1920s to the 1980s – first as Mark Antony in the Charles Doran Company, circa 1923, and lastly in No Man's Land, *1978 and* Early Days, *1981.*

Secondly, to have had the good fortune to make my first stage appearance with him in 1926 in Dear Brutus; *to have been his daughter again in* The Heiress *and his wife in* Lloyd George Knew My Father; *and finally his rejected sweetheart in* John Gabriel Borkman.

And thirdly, to be able to count myself a friend for over fifty years of one of the most extraordinary of actors and human beings.

Peggy Ashcroft

Sir Ralph can make an ordinary text sound like poetry by the music of his voice and the breath of his fantasy. Indeed, when he speaks it, it is poetry.

He can give rhythm and balance to ungainly prose. And he is the only actor who pronounces every syllable – sometimes it seems like every letter -- of a piece of dialogue. For a director, he is first and foremost a craftsman. He questions ceaselessly how to act. He knows, I am sure, that genius can only come once the craft is secure.

On the other hand, he makes the director's suggestions into gold with the speediness of all great actors. Any director who feels that he lacks originality in his ideas should try a few rehearsals with Sir Ralph. He will speedily feel a man of great imagination.

Sir Ralph exemplifies at the highest level, that genius in acting is not imitation but revelation – the revelation of the whole personality. As he has grown older he has revealed more and more of himself on the stage. And we have been able to wonder at the revelation not only of a great actor but of a great man.

Peter Hall   153

154

155

156

154 Nigel Havers, Alan Howard and Ralph Richardson in Jack Russell's *Comets among the Stars*, directed by Lionel Harris. ATV 1975. Richardson plays Professor Macleod whose life's work is destroyed when Banting discovers insulin.

155 Ralph Richardson as Simeon in *Jesus of Nazareth*, a film made for television, directed by Franco Zeffirelli. 1976.

156 James Caan and Ralph Richardson in *Rollerball*, a film set in the twenty-first century, directed by Norman Jewison. 1975. Richardson plays the Head Librarian.

157 Louis Jourdan and Ralph Richardson in Alexander Dumas' *The Man in the Iron Mask*, a film directed for television by Mike Newell. 1977. Richardson plays Colbert, one of the king's ministers.

157

I have always loved old actors ever since my first commercial success starred A.E. Matthews, who was in his eighties. Later, in a sequel to The Chiltern Hundreds, *Sybil Thorndike, also in her eighties, starred. For years, I looked back with nostalgia on both of them, since both were great performers and delightful people.*

Then, ten years or so ago, I met Sir Ralph. Compared to them, he was a juvenile, still in his early seventies. And yet I marked him down, at once, as their worthy successor. He had all the charm, the talent and the eccentricity that they had both been blessed with. Therefore, from the moment that I shook his hand across a table in the Ivy restaurant, I knew, instinctively, that I was back in business among my favourite age group.

The performance that he gave in Lloyd George Knew My Father *was inspired. His charm, his technique and his ever active intuition utterly transformed the character of General Sir William Boothroyd. Seldom can a playwright have secured a leading actor who fulfilled his wildest hopes to such a generous degree and turned what could have been a routine character into a work of art.*

Again in The Kingfisher, *his performance was a thing of beauty and the interplay between Dame Celia and Alan Webb and Ralph was a delight to watch.*

But, in that play as in the other, he was only in his seventies. And, as I tell him frequently, his best and most mature performances are yet to come.

A friend of mine went round to see him in his dressing-room during the run of his last play. 'When are you going to do another play of William's?' he enquired.

'My dear boy,' said Sir Ralph, his eyes a-twinkle and one eyebrow raised, 'He sends me one by every post.'

My inclination is to send them by hand in the future, if, by doing so, it will ensure a renewed partnership with an enchanting actor and an equally enchanting man.

William Douglas Home

158 Two lovers are re-united after fifty years. Ralph Richardson and Celia Johnson with Alan Webb in William Douglas Home's *The Kingfisher*, directed by Lindsay Anderson. Lyric Theatre, 1977.

159 'Life's gone on as if I'd never lived.' Ralph Richardson as Firs, the old footman, in Anton Chekhov's *The Cherry Orchard*, directed by Peter Hall. National Theatre, 1978.

160 Michael Jayston, Gary Bond, Ralph Richardson, Michael Gambon and Joanna Van Gysegham in *Alice's Boys*, by Felicity Browne and Jonathan Hales, directed by Lindsay Anderson. Savoy Theatre, 1978. Richardson plays the master-spy.

161 Robert Stephens as the villain, Maskwell, and Ralph Richardson as the cuckold, Lord Touchwood, in William Congreve's *The Double Dealer*, directed by Peter Wood. National Theatre, 1978.

159   *160*

*It's a well-known fact that Sir Ralph is magic
and by definition that is hardly something
one can describe. He has poetry in him and
when he reads Keats, for instance, you feel he
wrote it. He is beguiling and beady and
better in a big part than a small one. Which
is as it should be. He should always be seen.
He can invoke wonder and surprise,
simplicity and complicity, better than any
actor I know. He is privileged in his
extraordinary talent; and it is a privilege to
work with him and be near him.*

Dorothy Tutin

162 Ralph Richardson as Hirst and John Gielgud as Spooner in the Peter Hall National Theatre production of Harold Pinter's *No Man's Land*, directed for television by Julian Amyes. Granada Television 1978.

163

164

163 Brenda Blethyn and Ralph Richardson in Lev Tolstoy's *The Fruits of Enlightenment*, directed by Christopher Morahan. National Theatre, 1979. Richardson plays a rich landowner who is tricked into signing a contract which will allow the poor peasants to buy their land.

164 Michael Bryant, Stephen Moore, Eva Griffith and Ralph Richardson in Henrik Ibsen's *The Wild Duck*, directed by Christopher Morahan. National Theatre, 1979. Richardson plays Old Ekdal.

167

165 Ralph Richardson and David Hemmings in *Charlie Muffin*, directed by Jack Gold. Thames Television, 1979. Richardson plays Sir Archibald Willoughby.

166 Rosemary Martin and Ralph Richardson in David Storey's *Early Days*, directed by Lindsay Anderson. National Theatre, 1980. Transfers to Comedy Theatre and later to Toronto and Washington. Richardson plays a retired politician.

167 Ralph Richardson as the Supreme Being in *Time Bandits*, a film directed by Terry Gilliam. 1981.

168 Peter MacNicol as Galen and Ralph Richardson as Ulrich in *The Dragon Slayer*, a film directed by Matthew Robbins. 1982.

168

169

I first worked with Ralph Richardson in Alexander Korda's film, Things To Come, *nearly fifty years ago. I then admired an actor who had enormous energy and clarity and who dared. The dare succeeded and he gave a performance of splendid bravura.*

Now, all these years later, I have had the privilege of working with him in Angela Huth's The Understanding. *During that time, I realized that Ralph's greatness is his combination of artistry and craftsmanship. The ideas may come to him from God – but he works on them!*

His awareness of everything and everybody around him and his kindness and exceptional courtesy, garnished by his wondrous sense of humour, makes him, for me, not only a very great actor, but also a great man.

I salute him and love him!

Margaretta Scott

169 Margaretta Scott, Sylvestra Le Touzel and Ralph Richardson in Angela Huth's *The Understanding*, directed by Roger Smith. Strand Theatre, 1982. Richardson plays a man, who forty-five years too late, proposes to the woman he should have married.

170 Edward Judd and Ralph Richardson in the television production of David Storey's *Early Days*, directed by Anthony Page with Lindsay Anderson as consultant. 1982.

171 Ralph Richardson, Laurence Olivier and John Gielgud in *Wagner*, a film made for television, directed by Tony Palmer. 1983. Richardson plays Pfordten, a minister at the court of Ludwig II. Richard Burton plays Wagner.

170

I think the three outstanding actors of this time are Gielgud, Richardson and Olivier. I had the great good fortune to work with all three.

Please let the world know about an outstanding time in the English theatre.

Glen Byam Shaw

171

CHRONOLOGY
Plays

Date	Play	Role

1920-1921 St Nicholas Players, Brighton

Date	Play	Role
Jan	Jean Valjean	a gendarme
	The Farmer's Romance	Cuthbert
Mar	Macbeth	Banquo
		Macduff
May	The Moon-Children	Father
	The Taming of the Shrew	Tranio

1921 F.R. Crowcott Repertory Company, Brighton

Date	Play	Role
June	Twelfth Night	Malvolio
	The Taming of the Shrew	
July	The Farmer's Romance	Cuthbert
	Jean Valjean	a gendarme
	Waterloo	
	Oliver Twist	Mr Bumble
		Bill Sikes
	Macbeth	Banquo
		Macduff
Aug	A Tale of Two Cities	Defarge
		Stryver
		Marquis

1921/1923 Charles Doran Company, touring the provinces

Date	Play	Role
1921 Aug-Sep	The Merchant of Venice	Lorenzo
	Hamlet	Guildenstern
		Bernado
	The Taming of the Shrew	Pedant
	Julius Caesar	Soothsayer
		Strato
	As You Like It	Oliver
	Henry V	Scroop
		Gower
	Macbeth	Angus
		Macduff
	The Tempest	Francisco
	A Midsummer Night's Dream	Lysander
	Twelfth Night	Curio
		Valentine
1922 Jan-June	Macbeth	Banquo
	A Midsummer Night's Dream	Lysander
	Hamlet	Horatio
	Julius Caesar	Decius Brutus
		Octavius Caesar
	Twelfth Night	Fabian
	The Taming of the Shrew	Vincentio
Sep-Dec	The Taming of the Shrew	Lucentio
	Twelfth Night	Sebastian
1923 Jan-June	Othello	Cassio
	The Merchant of Venice	Antonio
		Gratiano
	Julius Caesar	Mark Antony

1923 Earle Grey Company, Abbey Theatre, Dublin

Date	Play	Role
July-Aug	The Rivals	Sir Lucius O'Trigger
	The Romantic Age	Bobby

Date	Play	Role	Theatre

1923-1924 Touring the provinces
1923 Sep-Nov	*Charles Doran Company*		
1924 Jan-June	Outward Bound	Henry	
Aug-Oct	The Way of the World	Fainall	
1925 Feb-Dec	The Farmer's Wife	Richard Coaker	

1925-1926 Birmingham Repertory Company
1925 Dec	The Christmas Party	Dick Whittington	
1926 Jan	The Cassilis Engagement	Geoffrey Cassilis	
Feb	The Round Table	Christopher Pegrum	
	He Who Gets Slapped	Gentleman	
Mar	The Importance of Being Earnest	Lane	
	Devonshire Cream	Robert Blanchard	
Apr	Hobson's Choice	Albert Prosser	
	Dear Brutus	Mr Dearth	
May	The Land of Promise	Frank Taylor	
Jun	The Barber and the Cow	Dr Tudor Bevan	

1926 Jul	Oedipus at Colonus	The Stranger	Scala
Aug	Devonshire Cream	Robert Blanchard	touring
Nov	Yellow Sands	Arthur Varwell	Haymarket

1927 Sunday Performances
Apr	Sunday Island	Harold Devrill	Strand
Jun	The Warden	John Bold	Royalty
Jul	Samson and Delilah	Sophus Meyer	Arts
Sep	Chance Acquaintance	Frank Liddell	Strand
Oct	At Number Fifteen	Albert Titler	Garrick

1928 Mar	Back to Methuselah	Zozim	Court
		Pygmalion	Court
Apr	Harold	Gurth	Court
	The Taming of the Shrew	Tranio	Court
Jun	Prejudice	Hezekiah Brent	Arts
Aug	Aren't Women Wonderful?	Ben Hawley	Court
Sep	The First Performance	Alexander Magnus	Court
Oct	The Runaways	James Jago	Garrick
Nov	The New Sin	David Llewellyn Davids	Epsom Little

1929 South African Tour: Gerald Lawrence's Company
Apr-Aug	Monsieur Beaucaire	Duke of Winterset	
	The School for Scandal	Joseph Surface	
	David Garrick	Squire Chivy	

1930 Feb	Silver Wings	Gilbert Nash	Dominion
	Cat and Mouse	Edward	Queen's
May	Othello	Roderigo	Savoy

1930-1931 The Old Vic Company
1930 Sep	Henry IV Part I	Henry	
Oct	The Tempest	Caliban	
	The Jealous Wife	Sir Harry Beagle	
Nov	Richard II	Bolingbroke	
1931 Jan	Twelfth Night	Sir Toby Belch	
Feb	Richard II	Bolingbroke	
	The Tempest	Caliban	

Date	Play	Role	Theatre
Mar	Arms and the Man	Bluntschli	
	Much Ado About Nothing	Don Pedro	
Apr	King Lear	Kent	
1931 May	The Mantle	David Regan	Arts

1931 Malvern Festival

Date	Play	Role	Theatre
1931 Aug	Ralph Roister Doister	Matthew Merrygreek	
	She Would If She Could	Mr Courtall	
	The Switchback	Viscount Pascal	

1931/1932 The Old Vic Company

Date	Play	Role	Theatre
1931 Sep	King John	Faulconbridge	
Oct	The Taming of the Shrew	Petruchio	
Nov	A Midsummer Night's Dream	Bottom	
Dec	Henry V	Henry	
1932 Jan	The Knight of the Burning Pestle	Ralph	
	Julius Caesar	Brutus	
Feb	Abraham Lincoln	General Grant	
Mar	Othello	Iago	
Apr	Twelfth Night	Sir Toby Belch	
	Hamlet	Ghost	
		First Grave-digger	

1932 Malvern Festival

Date	Play	Role	Theatre
Aug	Ralph Roister Doister	Merrygreek	
	The Alchemist	Face	
	Oroonoko	Oroonoko	
	Too True To Be Good	Sergeant Fielding	

Date	Play	Role	Theatre
1932 Sep	Too True To Be Good	Sergeant Fielding	New
Nov	For Services Rendered	Collie Stratton	Globe
1933 Feb	Head-on-Crash	Dirk Barclay	Queen's
May	Wild Decembers	Arthur Bell Nicholls	Apollo
Sep	Sheppey	Sheppey	Wyndham's
Dec	Peter Pan	Captain Hook	Palladium
		Mr Darling	
1934 Feb	Marriage Is No Joke	John MacGregor	Globe
Sep	Eden End	Charles Appleby	Duchess
1935 Mar	Cornelius	Cornelius	Duchess
Dec	Romeo and Juliet	Mercutio	Martin Beck, New York
		Chorus	
1936 Feb	Promise	Emile Delbar	Shaftesbury
May	Bees on the Boat Deck	Sam Gridley	Lyric
Aug	The Amazing Dr Clitterhouse	Dr Clitterhouse	Haymarket
1937 Nov	The Silent Knight	Peter Agardi	St James's
Dec	A Midsummer Night's Dream	Bottom	Old Vic
1938 Feb	Othello	Othello	Old Vic
1939 Feb	Johnson over Jordan	Johnson	New

1944-1947 The Old Vic Company at the New Theatre

Date	Play	Role	Theatre
1944 Aug	Peer Gynt	Peer	
Sep	Arms and the Man	Bluntschli	
	Richard III	Richmond	
1945 Jan	Uncle Vanya	Vanya	
Sep	Henry IV Parts I and II	Falstaff	
Oct	Oedipus	Tiresias	

Date	Play	Role	Theatre
	The Critic	Lord Burleigh	
1946 Oct	An Inspector Calls	Inspector Goole	
Nov	Cyrano de Bergerac	Cyrano	
1947 Jan	The Alchemist	Face	
Apr	Richard II	Gaunt	
The Company goes to the Comedie Francaise and Europe in 1945 and New York in 1946			
1948 Apr	Royal Circle	Marcus Ivanirex	Wyndham's
1949 Feb	The Heiress	Dr Sloper	Haymarket
1950 Mar	Home at Seven	David Preston	Wyndham's
1951 May	Three Sisters	Vershinin	Aldwych

1952 Shakespeare Memorial Theatre, Stratford-upon-Avon

Date	Play	Role	Theatre
1952 Mar-Oct	The Tempest	Prospero	
	Macbeth	Macbeth	
	Volpone	Volpone	
1953 Mar	The White Carnation	John Greenwood	Globe
Nov	A Day by the Sea	Dr Farley	Haymarket

1955 Tour of Australia and New Zealand

Date	Play	Role	Theatre
	The Sleeping Prince	Grand Duke	
	Separate Tables	Mr Martin	
		Major Pollock	
1956 Sep	Timon of Athens	Timon	Old Vic
1957 Jan	The Waltz of the Toreadors	General St Pé	New York
Nov	Flowering Cherry	Cherry	Haymarket
1959 Jun	The Complaisant Lover	Victor Rhodes	Globe
1960 Sep	The Last Joke	Edward Portal	Phoenix
1962 Apr	The School for Scandal	Sir Peter Teazle	Haymarket
1963 Jun	Six Characters in Search of an Author	Step-father	Mayfair

1964 British Council's Shakespeare Quatercentury Tour of South America and Europe

Date	Play	Role	Theatre
	The Merchant of Venice	Shylock	
	A Midsummer Night's Dream	Bottom	
1964 Sep	Carving a Statue	Father	Haymarket
1966 Jan	You Never Can Tell	William	Haymarket
Oct	The Rivals	Sir Anthony Absolute	Haymarket
1967 Sep	The Merchant of Venice	Shylock	Haymarket
1969 Mar	What The Butler Saw	Dr Rance	Queen's
1970 Jun	Home	Jack	Royal Court
1971 Aug	West of Suez	Wyatt Gilman	Royal Court
1972 July	Lloyd George Knew My Father	General Sir William Boothroyd	Savoy
1975 Jan	John Gabriel Borkman	Borkman	Old Vic
Apr	No Man's Land	Hirst	Old Vic
1977	The Kingfisher	Cecil	Lyric
1978 Feb	The Cherry Orchard	Firs	National
May	Alice's Boys	Colonel White	Savoy
Sep	The Double Dealer	Lord Touchwood	National
1979 Mar	The Fruits of Enlightenment	The Master	National
Dec	The Wild Duck	Old Ekdal	National
1980 Apr	Early Days	Kitchen	National
1982 May	The Understanding	Leonard	Strand

Films

(including films made for television)

1933	The Ghoul	Nigel Hartley
	Friday the Thirteenth	Schoolmaster
1934	The Return of Bulldog Drummond	Drummond
	Java Head	William Ammidon
	The King of Paris	Paul
1935	Bulldog Jack	Morrell
1936	Things To Come	The Boss
	The Man Who Could Work Miracles	Col. Winstanley
1937	Thunder in the City	Manningdale
1938	South Riding	Robert Carne
	The Divorce of Lady X	Lord Mere
	The Citadel	Dr Denny
	Smith	Smith
1939	Q Planes	Major Hammond
	The Four Feathers	Captain Durrance
	The Lion Has Wings	Wing-Commander
	On The Night of The Fire	Will Kobling
1942	The Day Will Dawn	Lockwood
1943	The Silver Fleet	Jaap Van Leyden
	The Volunteer	Himself
1946	School for Secrets	Professor Heatherville
1948	Anna Karenina	Karenin
	The Fallen Idol	Baines
1949	The Heiress	Dr Sloper
1951	An Outcast of the Islands	Captain Lingard
1952	Home at Seven	David Preston
	The Sound Barrier	John Richfield
	The Holly and The Ivy	The Rev. Gregory
1955	Richard III	Buckingham
1956	Smiley	The Rev. Lambeth
1957	The Passionate Stranger	Roger and Clement
1960	Our Man in Havana	'C'
	Oscar Wilde	Sir Edward Carson
	Exodus	General Sutherland
1962	The 300 Spartans	Themistocles
	Long Day's Journey Into Night	James Tyrone
1964	Woman of Straw	Charles Richmond
1965	Dr Zhivago	Alexander Gromeko
1966	Khartoum	Gladstone
	The Wrong Box	Joseph Finsbury
1969	Oh! What A Lovely War	Sir Edward Grey
	the bed-sitting room	Lord Fortnum
	Battle of Britain	David Kelly
	The Looking Glass War	Leclerc
	Midas Run	Henshaw
	David Copperfield	Micawber
1971	Whoever Slew Auntie Roo?	Mr Benton
	Eagle in a Cage	Sir Hudson Lowe
1972	Tales from the Crypt	Satan
	Alice's Adventures in Wonderland	Caterpillar
	Lady Caroline Lamb	George III
1973	A Doll's House	Dr Rank
	Dr Frankenstein: The True Story	Hermit
	O Lucky Man	Monty and Sir James Burgess
1975	Rollerball	Head Librarian
1976	Jesus of Nazareth	Simeon
1977	The Man in the Iron Mask	Colbert
1981	The Time Bandits	Supreme Being
1982	The Dragon Slayer	Ulrich
1983	Wagner	Pfordten
	Invitation to the Wedding	Bishop

Film Narrator

1940	Health for the Nation		1951	Cricket
	Forty Million People		1966	Chimes at Midnight
1949	Rome and Vatican City		1978	Watership Down
1950	Eagles of the Fleet			

Television Plays

1962	Hedda Gabler	Judge Brack	BBC-CBS
	Heart to Heart	Sir Stanley Johnson	BBC
1963	Voices of Man		America
1965	Johnson Over Jordan	Robert Johnson	BBC
1966	Blandings Castle	Clarence, 9th Earl of	
		Emsworth	BBC
1968	Twelfth Night	Sir Toby Belch	ATV
1970	Hassan	Hassan	BBC
	She Stoops To Conquer	Mr Hardcastle	BBC
1972	Home	Jack	BBC
1975	Comets Among The Stars	Professor Macleod	ATV
1978	No Man's Land	Hirst	Granada TV
1979	Charlie Muffin	Sir Archibald Willoughby	Thames Television
1982	Early Days	Kitchen	Terence Donovan/
			Consolidated Productions

Radio

Ralph Richardson makes his first broadcast on 7 March 1929 in 'The City'. The chronology which follows is selective.

1929	The City	1946	Moby Dick
	Twelfth Night	1947	Rubaiyat of Omar Khayyam
	Captain Brassbound's Conversion	1949	Brand
1931	The Tempest	1953	A Midsummer Night's Dream
1932	Romeo and Juliet	1958	Noah
1933	Macbeth	1960	Richard II
	The Tempest	1961	Hamlet
	Julius Caesar		Arms and the Man
1934	A Midsummer Night's Dream	1963	The Ballad of Reading Gaol
1935	Through The Looking Glass		The Merchant of Venice
1936	In Memoriam	1964	Christmas Carol
	The Tempest	1966	Cyrano de Bergerac
1937	Candida	1968	Heartbreak House
1940	Johnson over Jordan	1969	When We Dead Awaken
1941	Job		Much Ado About Nothing
1942	The Shoemaker's Holiday	1974	John Gabriel Borkman
	Dr Faustus	1976	The Phoenix and the Turtle
1943	Don Quixote		The Passionate Pilgrim
1944	Peer Gynt	1977	Programme on William Blake
1945	Cyrano de Bergerac	1978	Readings from Andrew Marvell
	Henry IV Parts I and II	1982	Little Tich – Giant of the Halls

ACKNOWLEDGEMENTS

(all figures refer to caption numbers)
The author and publisher would like to express their appreciation to the following for their assistance and/or permission to reproduce the photographs. Every effort has been made to trace copyright owners and the author and publishers would like to apologise to anyone whose copyright has unwittingly been infringed.

ATV Network Ltd 128, 154; BBC Copyright 116, 117, 126, 138, 139, 143; BBC Hulton Picture Library 32, 136, 137, 142, 172; The Birmingham Reference Library 36; The Birmingham Repertory Theatre 3, 4, 8; BFI National Film Archive/Stills Library 27, 29, 30, 31, 35, 37, 38, 41, 43, 46, 47, 49, 53, 54, 55, 56, 57, 58, 59, 78, 79, 81, 82, 84, 88, 89, 93, 94, 100, 101, 104, 108, 109, 112, 113, 114, 115, 119, 121, 122, 123, 129, 131, 132, 133, 134, 135, 140, 141, 144, 145, 148, 149, 150, 151, 156, 157; Columbia-Warner 108, 123, 150, 151; Connoisseur 114, 115; Donald Cooper 163; Anthony Crickmay 153; Terence Donovan/Consolidated Productions 170; Zoë Dominic 152, 159, 164; EMI 30, 31, 81, 82, 88, 89, 93, 94, 100, 104, 133, 146, 148; Financial Times 160; Granada TV 162; Handmade Films 167; Harris Films/Kingston (Robert) Films 46; John Haynes 161, 166; Hemdale Films/Southbrook Films 140; Peter Hirst 169; Illustrated London News Library 40, 44; ITC Entertainment Ltd 157; London Films 37, 38, 41, 47, 53, 54, 55, 79; London Trust Cultural Productions Ltd 171; The Lowestoft Reference Library 1; Raymond Mander and Joe Mitchenson Theatre Collection 20, 28; MCA TV 149; Angus McBean, Harvard Theatre Collection 50, 51, 52, 80, 86, 87, 90, 91, 92, 95, 96, 97, 98, 99, 102, 105, 106, 107, 110, 111, 120, 124, 125, 130; MGM 49, 121; National General Pictures 141; Maurice Newcombe 118; Paramount 84, 129; Rank Organisation 27, 29, 35, 56, 57, 58, 78, 131, 144; Houston Rogers (Victoria and Albert Museum, Crown Copyright) 83, 85, 127; Ralph Richardson 2, 9, 12, 14, 21; The Shakespeare Birthplace Trust 17; Thames Television Copyright Frontispiece, 165; Theatre Museum Frontispiece, 5, 6, 7, 10, 11, 13, 16, 18, 19, 22, 23, 24, 25, 26, 34, 39, 42, 45, 48; Times Newspapers Ltd 15, 103; Twentieth Century Fox 101, 109, 113, 135, 145; United Artists 33, 43, 112, 119, 122, 132, 134, 156; John Vickers 60 to 77 inclusive; Walt Disney Ltd 168; Reg Wilson 147, 158.

The author would like to add an additional note of thanks to Sir Ralph and Lady Richardson; everybody at the Theatre Museum; The Stills and Reference Library of the BFI; the press office of The Birmingham Repertory Theatre; the press office of the National Theatre; H.M. Tennent Ltd; Peter Hirst; Mavis Quinault; and Mrs John Vickers.